NATURE CUTS

NATURE CUTS

A Collection of Over 20 Beautiful Papercutting Projects and Templates

GEORGIA LOW

HERBERT PRESS

LONDON · OXFORD · NEW YORK · NEW DELHI · SYDNEY

HERBERT PRESS
Bloomsbury Publishing Plc
50 Bedford Square, London, WC1B 3DP,
UK

BLOOMSBURY, HERBERT PRESS and
the Herbert Press logo are trademarks of
Bloomsbury Publishing Plc

First published in Great Britain 2018

A catalogue record for this book is
available from the British Library

ISBN: PB: 978-1-9122-1733-5;
eBook: 978-1-9122-1736-6

2 4 6 8 10 9 7 5 3 1

Printed in China

To find out more about our authors and
books visit www.bloomsbury.com and
sign up for our newsletters

QUAR.PCFW

Conceived, designed, and produced by
Quarto Publishing plc, an imprint of
The Quarto Group, 6 Blundell Street,
London N7 9BH

Editor: Kate Burkett
Senior art editor: Emma Clayton
Designer: Emily Portnoi
Photography: Dave Burton,
Jess Esposito, and Phil Wilkins
Art director: Caroline Guest
Creative director: Moira Clinch
Publisher: Samantha Warrington

CONTENTS

MEET GEORGIA

My name's Georgia and I'm a professional papercut artist working and living in beautiful North Wales with my partner Tom and our Cockapoo Millie.

For as long as I can remember, I have always been a lover of art and there was something so relaxing and therapeutic about sitting down with a piece of paper and sketching out my ideas – much to our fridge's dismay! I suppose that's why I fell in love with the art of papercutting – you can sit there for hours cutting away, but it feels like you're in another world. Plus, you end up with something beautiful at the end!

I work from my studio at home with my puppy, Millie. Admittedly she has eaten a few offcuts of paper, but she gets away with most things because she looks like a teddy bear! In my spare time we go for walks through the fields near our house and drink a lot of tea, but my main hobby is my work. I easily spend hours creating new ideas and planning out commissions for my clients. My love of the surrounding countryside, flowers and wild animals has definitely influenced the majority of my art. And I hope that they fill people with as much joy as they do for me making them.

One of my favourite papercuts has to be my Amsterdam piece (right). I love it so much that I couldn't bear to part with it, so it's sitting nicely in my studio.

I created this piece (left) for a solo exhibition I held for a big company in London. As with most of my art, this papercut was inspired by nature. The hare was such fun to draw. I wanted to create a sense of movement in the piece and the hardest part to cut was definitely all of the tiny hairs!

EQUIPMENT&
TECHNIQUES

TOOLS AND MATERIALS

You really don't need a huge arsenal of tools to get going with papercutting, but there are definitely some tools that will make your life easier and your cutting neater.

PAPER

If you are new to papercutting, buy a selection of different papers that appeal to you, take them home and have a go at cutting them. Try small and big shapes; long, sweeping cuts; and tiny, intricate cuts.

Weight

When thinking about paper weight, consider your design. For example, if you are creating a 3-D piece, you may want to opt for a heavier card – 160gsm (60lb) upwards – as you will need more rigidity than a lighter weight could give you. You'll find weight suggestions on each project page, but I advise you to choose 120–200gsm (40–80lb).

10-11 Carbon paper

Carbon paper is an excellent material to use when transferring your template design. It is available in a few colours, but black and white are the most common. This paper can be reused multiple times, so you don't need to buy a lot of it.

12 Coloured paper

The colours you choose not only have an impact on the finished look of your papercut project, but also on how you will transfer the template to your card (see *Transferring your Design*, page 14).

EQUIPMENT

1 Metal safeguard ruler

A metal ruler is best, as your blade would easily cut into a plastic or wooden one, leaving an uneven edge.

2 Needle holder

Needle holders are useful when it comes to handling the blades of your craft knife (see *Using Craft Knives*, page 16).

3-4 Craft knives

Sometimes referred to as a scalpel, a craft knife is the most important tool. There are many models to choose from, but the most well-known makes are X-Acto, Swann Morton and Fiskars. Pick a handle that's light and feels comfortable in your grip.

5 Pencil

As well as your standard pencil, I would also recommend purchasing a white pencil, as it is useful for drawing on dark paper.

6-7 Craft screw punch

Often used for book binding, a screw punch is used to create neat and uniformly sized holes in paper and card. Look for a model that comes with various-sized attachments (6).

8 Bone folder

A bone folder is a butter-knife-shaped tool made of plastic, which is run along the edge of your ruler to create a fold line in the paper. It will help you to create really neat and clean folds.

9 Cutting mat

There are many different types of cutting mat, but the best is a self-healing mat. It has a special non-slip and non-reflective surface, meaning that you have total control over your scalpel when cutting your templates.

ADDITIONAL TOOLS

Glue
Masking tape
Double-sided sticky tape or sticky pads
Guillotine

TRANSFERING YOUR DESIGN

The templates can be used as they appear in this book (see pages 78–125). Just tear along the perforated edges, cutting out the grey shaded areas to reveal your design. If, however, you don't want to cut up your book or would like to reuse your templates, there are other ways to transfer your designs to paper.

If you'd like to reuse the templates, I would suggest scanning them into your computer before cutting. This way, you can print off as many as you like, which is especially useful for projects such as the Butterfly Wall Art (pages 52–53), Bear Bunting (pages 54–55) and Succulents (pages 72–73). Alternatively, you can trace the template with tracing paper.

If you have a printer, you can print the projects directly onto your chosen paper so that you don't have to use up a template or trace your design. Most printers will only work with paper that is between 75gsm and 160gsm (20lb and 60lb). Simply print out as many copies of your template as you want, and get cutting! You can also download the templates so they can be used again and again.

DOWNLOAD YOUR TEMPLATES HERE
www.quartoknows.com/page/naturecutstemplates.

USING CARBON PAPER

I like to use black and white carbon paper as it allows you to transfer your design to any colour paper that you'd like to cut from. For example, you would use white carbon paper for darker colours, where normal pencil marks would barely show, and black carbon paper for lighter colours.

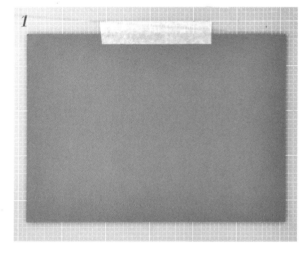

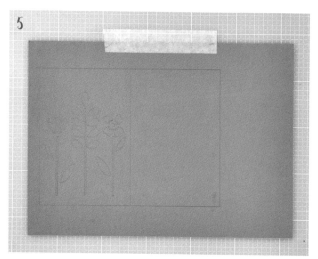

1. Take your chosen card and carefully stick one of the edges onto your cutting mat, using masking tape.

2. Gently position a sheet of carbon paper on top of the card, carbon side down. Be careful not to move the carbon paper or put any pressure on it just yet, as it can easily transfer the carbon. Place another piece of tape on the edges to hold the carbon paper in place.

3. Place your template over the carbon paper and tape it down, making sure both are secure.

4. Using a pencil, trace over the template lines. Your pencil lines will be transferred onto your card. You could even modify the design as you go, if desired.

5. Remove the printed template and the carbon paper to reveal the design on the card. You can now go over any sections that are less visible, if needed.

USING CRAFT KNIVES

The craft knife, often referred to as a scalpel, is your most important papercutting tool. It is important to replace the blades regularly so that you can achieve clean cuts – here's how!

CHANGING YOUR BLADES: CRAFT KNIVES SUCH AS X-ACTO

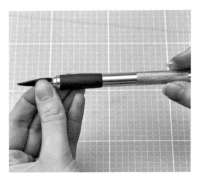

1. Carefully hold the back of the blade at its base.

2. With your other hand, twist the handle clockwise to release the blade.

3. Simply slot the new blade in place and twist the handle anti-clockwise until it is rigid.

The most common way to hold your knife is to hold it as you would a pencil or pen, resting the craft knife handle between your thumb and index finger. The cushioned section of the handle should be resting on your middle finger, while you control the top of the handle with your index finger sitting on top and your thumb to the side.

CHANGING YOUR BLADES: SWANN MORTON CRAFT KNIVES

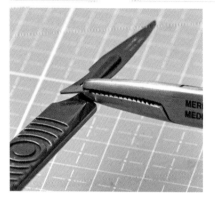

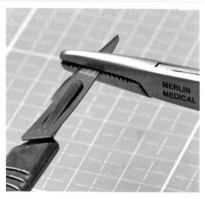

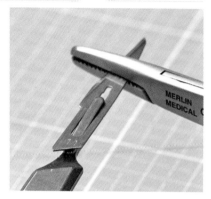

1. Hold your craft knife blade at the base with a needle holder, making sure that the blade end is facing away from you.

2. Carefully lift up the base of the blade slightly so that it is just a bit higher than the central ridge on which it sits.

3. Hold the tip of the blade with the needle holder and pull slowly until the blade slips off. Safely discard the old blade.

TO PLACE A NEW BLADE ONTO YOUR SWANN MORTON HANDLE

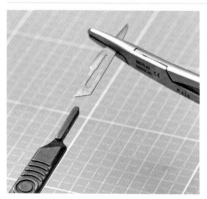

1. Sandwich the tip of the blade between the blades of your needle holder.

2. At a slight angle, slot the new blade into the small gap in the handle. Make sure that the base of the blade goes over the top of the ridge.

3. Keep pushing the blade until it clicks into place.

DIRECTION OF CUT

The direction of your cut is extremely important, and heavily impacts on the quality of your finished papercut. I learned through trial and error that there is a rule to cutting out negative shapes, particularly those with delicate sections. You need to make sure that the delicate parts do not deform and curl, which can separate the layers of the paper and give an untidy finish.

NEGATIVE SHAPES

1. With your template on the cutting mat, place the tip of your blade on the top of the pointed shape.

2. Pull your blade downwards, towards the base of the grey area, to create the edge.

3. Move your blade back to the first point. Now pull your blade down the other side until it reaches the next base point.

4. Repeat on the other side, then repeat this process until all of the points have been cut.

5. Cut along the bottom line to remove the shape.

Positive space

Negative space

1. Place the tip of your blade at the base of the grey area and pull towards the first point of the shape.

2. Now place your blade at the next lower point, and cut upwards to meet the last point.

3. Repeat these steps until all of the points have been cut.

4. Finally, cut out the rest of the grey area, swivelling your paper to cut out the curves.

5. Remove the shape.

HOW TO READ A PAPERCUT

The beauty of papercutting lies in how your eyes read the design: the art of seeing the overall pattern over the mass of detail. Take this flower, for example: once the grey areas have been cut away, you will be left with windows within the petals. The windows are called negative space; the flower papercut that is left is called positive space.

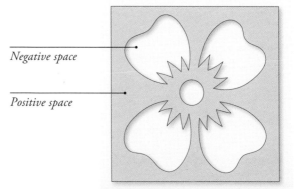

Negative space

Positive space

CUTTING TECHNIQUES

CIRCLE-CUTTING TECHNIQUES

When papercutting, you often have to cut circles. Here are my go-to circle-cutting techniques, which should help you cut out these often problematic shapes in style!

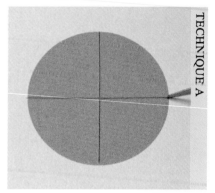

TECHNIQUE A

1. Start with your template on your cutting mat and a new blade in your craft knife. Cut a line across the circle.

2. Turn your paper 90 degrees and cut another line across the circle to create a plus sign.

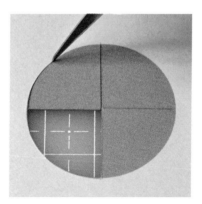

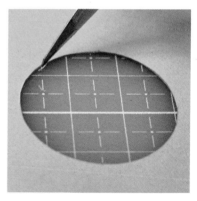

3. Cut out each quarter individually by slowly turning the paper as you go, or curving your blade around the outside of the shape. Continue until all the quarters have been removed.

4. You can now neaten up the circle if necessary by carefully trimming small sections.

1. Place the tip of your blade on the edge of your circle. Slowly pull the blade along the line towards you in one smooth motion.

2. With the blade in the paper, hold it still, carefully swivel your paper slightly, then continue cutting. Keeping the blade in the paper when you turn it ensures you don't restart cutting in the wrong place, which would give a messy finish.

3. Continue swivelling the paper and cutting until you can remove the circle. Neaten up the circle, cutting tiny sections away.

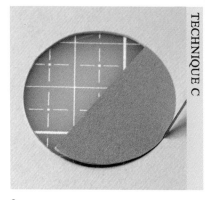

1. With your template on your cutting mat, start by cutting a straight line across the circle from left to right.

2. Place the tip of your blade at the left point of the cut line and, in one smooth motion, pull the knife along the edge of the circle, curving the blade slightly until you reach the right cut line. Remove this half of the circle.

3. Repeat Step 2 on the other side until both halves are cut out and removed. Neaten up if necessary.

USING A SCREW PUNCH AND SCORING AND FOLDING

These tools will make the papercutting process (and your life) much easier.

USING A SCREW PUNCH

This is sometimes called a Japanese or bookbinding punch and is used for creating uniform holes in paper and card. Look for a model that comes with a few attachments for making holes of different sizes.

1. Decide which size of bit to use for the hole you would like to cut by placing it over the circle.

2. Place the bit inside the screw punch, using the same method as for your standard craft knife (see page 16).

3. Line up your screw punch with the circle.

4. Once you're happy with the position, press down the screw punch and remove.

SCORING AND FOLDING

A metal ruler and bone folder are your best friends when it comes to folding. Use them to score a crease line down the paper as a guide to where to fold. This will prevent the paper from creasing, splitting or tearing when you fold it.

1. Place your template onto your cutting mat, or another smooth and flat surface. Hold your ruler flat against the dashed line. With your bone folder, carefully press and pull it along the ruler as you would with a pencil.

2. Fold your paper along the line. You can use the flat back of your bone folder to press down along the fold, giving a neater crease in the paper.

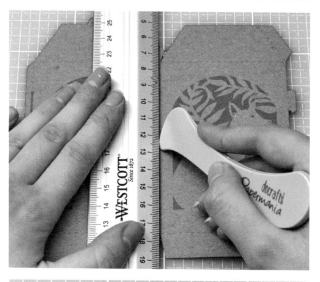

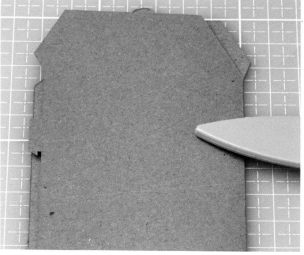

FRAMING

There are many different ways to frame your papercut, each of which gives a different feel to the piece of art. My go-to method, however, is to use a floating frame.

FLOATING FRAME

A beautiful way of framing your papercut is by 'floating' it, which suspends it between two sheets of glass, so that you can see the dimension and shadows your design creates.

1. Open up your frame and remove the top sheet of glass, leaving the bottom sheet in place.

2. Now place your papercut face down in the centre of the glass. If preferred, you can do this on your cutting mat, using the lines as a guide to make sure it's straight and central.

3. Carefully place the second sheet of glass on top to sandwich the papercut.

4. Reposition the insert on top of the glass. If your frame doesn't have a backboard, secure the tabs. If it does have a backboard, place a sheet of coloured card (cut to size), so that it's resting on the edges of the insert.

6. Finally, place the backboard down and secure the tabs.

THE PROJECTS

PROJECT FINDER

This chapter features over 20 beautiful papercutting projects to test all skill levels.
Start off with the Toadstool gift tag and work your way up to the Happy floral hare.

WILDFLOWER CARD: *page 32*

HAPPY FLORAL HARE: *page 34*

FRAMED FERN: *page 38*

LEAF FAVOUR BOX: *page 40*

PEONY FRAME: *page 42*

GOLD LEAF GARLAND: *page 44*

RED SQUIRREL: *page 16*

HONEYCOMB BOOKMARK: *page 18*

SIMPLE FLOWER TRIO CARD: *page 50*

BUTTERFLY WALL ART: *page 52*

BEAR BUNTING: *page 54*

BIRD AND FEATHER MOBILE: *page 56*

CAKE TOPPER: *page 58*

FEATHER PLACE NAME: *page 60*

FOX AND HARE LANTERN: *page 62*

LAYERED STAGE ARTWORK: *page 66*

FLOWER PICTURE: *page 68*

HUMMINGBIRD GLASS DECORATION: *page 70*

SUCCULENTS: *page 72*

BEE PAPERCUT: *page 74*

TOADSTOOL GIFT TAG: *page 76*

WILDFLOWER CARD

This stunning design will help to hone your craft-knife skills. Beautifully elegant, this wildflower design is sure to brighten someone's day.

TOOLS

• Craft knife
• Cutting mat
• Bone folder
• Metal ruler
• Spray adhesive

MATERIALS

• Card for the flowers, 160gsm (60lb)
• Card for the insert, maximum 160gsm (60lb)
• Length of ribbon, approximately 2cm (¾in) wide (optional)

Template on page 81

1. Download and print the Wildflower Card template onto your chosen card, or use one of the other methods on pages 14–15 to transfer or trace the design.

2. Cut the smaller sections in between the stems, as these are the most fragile parts of the flowers.

3. Turn the template upside down to cut the outline of the thistle. Cut from the middle of the thistle outwards and towards you to create the points.

4. Cut the outlines of the flowers, turning the card to cut the curves rather than trying to bend your hand.

5. Finally, cut along the outside lines to create the borders.

6. Using the bone folder and the ruler, score along the dashed lines and fold each edge over to the centre of the card, creating a double-door effect. Press down on the folds with the bone folder to create sharp creases.

7. Write or print your message onto the coloured card of your choice. Trim the insert to approximately 148 x 210mm – A5 size (5¾ x 8¼in).

8. Lay the insert face down on some scrap card and spray the back lightly with spray adhesive. Carefully position the insert on the inside panel of your card and leave it to dry.

9. Fold the doors back in to meet in the middle. If using ribbon, wrap it around the centre of the card and tie it in a bow at the front.

HAPPY FLORAL HARE

This leaping hare is full of the joys of spring, and looks great in a frame. The intricate-looking design is made from lots of large shapes, so it is much easier to cut than it appears to be.

TOOLS

- Craft knife
- Cutting mat
- Spray adhesive

MATERIALS

- Card for the hare, 160gsm (60lb)
- Card for the background, minimum 160gsm (60lb)
- 22 x 28-cm (8½ x 11-in) frame

1. Download and print the Happy Floral Hare template onto your chosen card, or use one of the other methods on pages 14–15 to transfer or trace the design.

2. Cut out all of the circles, turning the card rather than bending the knife.

3. To cut the ears, start from the top and work your way down, so that you don't snag any fragile sections of cut card.

4. Carry on cutting down to the front legs and work your way to the back.

5. Now that you have finished cutting the hare, you can either leave it unglued, to be framed 'floating', or move on to the next step.

6. Place the hare face down on a sheet of scrap card and spray with spray adhesive.

7. Carefully pick up the hare and place it glue side down in the desired position on your background card.

8. Finally, place your finished picture face down in the frame, and secure. Now it is ready to hang up.

Template on page 83

When coming up with the design for the Happy Floral Hare, I decided to take some inspiration from one of my favourite papercuts (top, right). My original piece featured a whimsical leaping hare surrounded by a border of flowers and leaves. I knew I wanted to make something similar, but with the flowers incorporated more into the shape of the animal. First, I sketched a rough outline of the leaping hare. Then, once I was happy with the overall shape, I carefully drew all of the flowers and leaves to fit within the hare and erased the outline.

CREATING CARROTS

Instead of wasting any scraps of leftover paper, you could create beautiful mini designs from your offcuts. I decided to make some small carrots to accompany the Happy Floral Hare.

1. Lightly draw your carrot shapes on your leftover paper. When drawing the leaves, I find it best if they are joined up in multiple places; this makes them easier to cut and also stops the carrots from becoming too fragile.

2. Once you are happy with your carrot shapes, start by cutting around the leaves. Make sure you cut the smaller inner sections out first.

3. Cut out the small thin lines that go across your carrot. Place the tip of your blade on one of the points and carefully pull the blade to the next. Go back to the first point with your blade and repeat underneath, ensuring your cut is a couple of millimetres wide.

4. Finally, cut along the outline of your carrot, starting from around the leaves as this is the most fragile section.

FRAMED FERN

This attractive fern leaf design with its points and delicate lines will test your cutting skills. Cut out different shades of green for a statement display. Frame the fern leaves in a zinc or copper frame for a stylish twist.

TOOLS

• Craft knife

• Cutting mat

• Double-sided sticky foam pads (for zinc frame) or spray adhesive (for frame of your choice)

MATERIALS

• Card for the fern, 120–160gsm (50–60lb)

• 20 x 25-cm (8 x 10-in) zinc frame or frame of your choice

1. Download and print the Framed Fern template onto your chosen card, or use one of the other methods on pages 14–15 to transfer or trace the design.

2. Begin by cutting out all of the grey sections in the leaf.

3. Starting at the tip of the fern, cut along the outline, turning the card as you work so that the tips of the smaller leaves are always facing towards you.

4. Work your way down the leaf until the design is complete. Carefully remove the leaf from the surrounding card.

5. If using a zinc frame, place a couple of double-sided sticky foam pads on the back of the fern and place the fern directly into your frame. Secure, and hang on your wall. Alternatively, spray the back of your leaf with adhesive and mount it onto another sheet of card. Secure in your choice of frame.

Template on page 85

LEAF FAVOUR BOX

This favour box is simple to create, but makes a big impression. Use colours that match your place settings for a unique way to present favours to your guests.

TOOLS

- Metal ruler
- Bone folder
- Craft knife
- Cutting mat
- Spray adhesive

MATERIALS

- Twine or ribbon, maximum 5mm (⅕in) wide
- Card for the box, 160gsm (60lb)

1. Download and print the Leaf Favour Box template onto your chosen card, or use one of the other methods on pages 14–15 to transfer or trace the design. Using your ruler and bone folder, score along all of the dotted lines.

2. Starting from the middle of the leaf, carefully cut out the grey sections, working your way outwards to reveal the full design.

3. Now cut out the small holes, turning the card regularly to achieve a smooth, circular cut.

4. Cut out the thin rectangles; your tabs will slot into these when the box is folded.

5. Change your blade now if it is starting to blunt, then move on to cutting along all of the solid lines, including the tabs.

6. Carefully fold along the lines you scored earlier.

7. Starting with the base, slot the tabs into the rectangular holes, then move on to the sides, and finally the top section.

8. Lastly, place your chosen favour(s) in the box, thread your ribbon or twine through both of the holes and tie it in a bow.

Template on page 81

PEONY FRAME

Take the opportunity to frame a special memory with this stunning peony papercut. Simply place your chosen photograph in the middle for a thoughtful keepsake for yourself or a loved one.

TOOLS

• Craft knife
• Cutting mat
• Metal ruler
• Glue stick or glue pen
• Spray adhesive

MATERIALS

• Card for the peony border
• Card for the background
• 20 x 25-cm (8 x 10-in) frame

Template on page 89

1. Download and print the Peony Frame template onto your chosen card, or use one of the other methods on pages 14–15 to transfer or trace the design.

2. Starting at the top of the template, cut out the grey shaded areas of the top three peonies. These are quite detailed, so it is best to get them out of the way first to reduce the chance of tearing.

3. Now cut out the grey areas inside the surrounding leaves. The points joined to the central line are fragile, so be sure to cut them from tip to base.

4. Cut out the grey areas in between the flowers and leaves, using your ruler to cut along the straight edges of the shapes.

5. Continue to cut out the design down the sides of the frame, turning the card when cutting out the curves of the berries.

6. Finish the border by cutting out the last section of the peonies and leaves. Then, using your ruler and craft knife, cut out the grey rectangle in the centre.

7. Print off your chosen photograph and, if necessary, trim to 8.5 x 10.5cm (3⅓ x 4in).

8. Using your glue stick or glue pen, stick the inner edge of the papercut and your photograph in place, face down.

9. Move your papercut onto a scrap piece of card and spray with adhesive. Finally, stick your papercut to the middle of the background card and secure in your frame.

GOLD LEAF GARLAND

These delicate gold leaves are an ideal way to decorate a room for a special occasion. You can hang them individually or string several together to make an eye-catching garland.

TOOLS

- Craft knife
- Cutting mat
- Hole or screw punch (optional)

MATERIALS

- Coloured card, 120–300gsm (50–110lb)
- String or ribbon, maximum 4mm (⅛in) wide

1. Download and print the Gold Leaf Garland templates onto your chosen card, or use one of the other methods on pages 14–15 to transfer or trace the design.

2. Choose a leaf design and, using a craft knife on a cutting mat, begin cutting out the grey areas, cutting downwards from the stem.

3. Work your way down the leaf until all of the grey areas have been cut out.

4. Now cut out the hole at the top of the stem. This can be done with your craft knife, or with a hole or screw punch if preferred.

5. Cut around the outline of the leaf and remove it from the surrounding card.

6. Repeat Steps 1–5 to complete the other two leaves, and repeat as necessary depending on how long you would like your garland to be.

7. Lastly, thread your leaves onto your string or ribbon for hanging as individual decorations, or in an alternating pattern onto string or ribbon cut to the required length for a garland.

Templates on page 91

RED SQUIRREL

A fantastic way to practise cutting curves and small details, this squirrel design will take some time and patience to cut, but it is well worth the effort, resulting in a beautiful piece of art to cherish for years to come.

TOOLS

- Craft knife
- Cutting mat
- Spray adhesive (optional)

MATERIALS

- Card for the squirrel
- Card for the background (optional)
- Frame (optional)

1. Download and print the Red Squirrel template onto your chosen card, or use one of the other methods on pages 14–15 to transfer or trace the design.

2. With your template on the cutting mat, start by cutting out the grey areas on the main body of the squirrel and the acorn.

3. Using one of the circle-cutting techniques shown on pages 20–21, cut out all of the circles within the floral design of the tail. These are found in the middle of the flowers.

4. Cut out all of the petals that make up the three biggest flowers, cutting the points from base to tip to avoid damaging the card.

5. Now, all of the fragile sections have been cut out. Work your way through the rest of the design, cutting from the top of the tail downwards.

6. Cut along the line around the outside of the squirrel and remove the design from your sheet of card.

7. If you are framing the design, cut your background card to the desired size.

8. Place the squirrel on a scrap piece of card and spray with adhesive. Now place the squirrel glue side down on your background card and frame.

Template on page 93

HONEYCOMB BOOKMARK

A colourful bookmark to make sure that you never lose your place again! This template will require some precision, and will show you how to work with layers. It would make the perfect gift for an avid book reader or bee lover.

TOOLS

- Craft knife
- Cutting mat
- Glue stick or glue pen
- Spray adhesive

MATERIALS

- Card for the bookmark
- Card for the background
- Yellow card
- White card
- String or ribbon, maximum 4mm (⅛in) wide

Templates on page 95

1. Download and print the Honeycomb Bookmark templates onto your chosen card, or use one of the other methods on pages 14–15 to transfer or trace the design.

2. Cut out the small grey areas inside and surrounding the bees, including the eyes and the hexagons around the antennae.

3. Cut out the small semi-circle and the rest of the honeycomb, starting from the top of the bookmark and working your way down until the design is complete.

4. Now that your bookmark design is almost complete, move on to the next section of the template and cut out all of the shapes from yellow or white card, as appropriate. These shapes will make up the yellow parts of the bees, the hexagons and the white wings.

5. Using your glue stick or glue pen, place a small amount of glue on the lower bodies of the bees and stick the leaf-like shapes in place, yellow side down. Then carefully glue the template around the wings of the bees and stick the white shapes in place.

6. Glue around the hexagon directly above the top bee's left wing and stick the matching incomplete yellow hexagon in place. Then glue around the hexagon directly above the second bee's head and stick the other yellow hexagon in place.

7. Now decide where you would like your last four yellow hexagons to go and glue these in place.

8. Cut along the outline of the bookmark and the matching outline for the background. Remove these from the surrounding card.

9. Place your bookmark on a scrap piece of card and spray with adhesive. Then line up your background card and fix it in place.

10. Finally, thread the string or ribbon through the semi-circle, tie and cut to the desired length.

SIMPLE FLOWER TRIO CARD

Send a message or invite a loved one to a special occasion with this simple yet graphic card. This retro-inspired card will look stunning in a sunny spot with the sun casting beautiful shadows onto the paper insert.

TOOLS

• Craft knife
• Cutting mat
• Metal ruler
• Bone folder
• Glue stick or double-sided tape

MATERIALS

• Paper for the card, minimum 160gsm (60lb)
• Paper for the insert

1. Download and print the Simple Flower Trio Card template onto your chosen paper. Alternatively, use one of the other methods on pages 14–15 to transfer or trace the design.

2. Starting with the flower on the left, cut out the grey circles and the curved stems underneath them. Finally, cut out the two leaves on either side of the stem.

3. Now cut out the leaves on the middle flower. Place the tip of your blade in the middle of the curve and pull the blade around and down in one motion until you reach the tip of the leaf. Repeat on the other side to complete, and remove the shape.

4. Cut out the grey circle in the middle of the final flower, followed by the petals and the leaves. Next, using your craft knife and ruler, cut out all of the stems.

5. Using your ruler and bone folder, score along the dashed line. Now use your ruler and craft knife to cut around the edge of the card.

6. Turn the card over and fold it in half. Fold the paper you have chosen for the insert in half and trim the unfolded edges slightly with a ruler and craft knife to fit.

7. Finally, spread a line of glue or attach a strip of double-sided tape inside the card against the fold and stick the insert in place.

Template on page 91

BUTTERFLY WALL ART

Practise your curves with these delicate 3-D butterflies. Repeat the templates multiple times to create a statement on your wall, or stick down the butterflies, in the shape of your choice, on backing paper, and display them in a box frame.

TOOLS

• Cutting mat
• Craft knife
• Double-sided sticky foam pads
• Bone folder
• Metal ruler

MATERIALS

• Card for the butterflies, 120–160gsm (50–60lb)

1. Download and print the Butterfly Wall Art templates onto your chosen card, or use one of the other methods on pages 14–15 to transfer or trace the design.

2. Place your template on your cutting mat and choose which of the six butterflies you'd like to start with.

3. Begin by cutting out the grey shaded areas at the top of the butterfly. Place the tip of your blade in the middle of the curve and pull the blade around and down until you reach the tip of the shape. Repeat on the other side to complete, and remove the section.

4. Repeat with the rest of the grey areas inside the design until all of them have been cut out.

5. Starting with the antennae, cut along the outside line of the butterfly and remove it from the sheet of card.

6. Trim your sticky foam pads to fit the body of the butterfly. Peel off the film from one side of the foam and stick it in place.

7. Now, using your bone folder and ruler, score along the dashed lines. Turn the butterfly over and gently fold the wings upwards.

8. Finally, remove the film from the back of the foam and stick the butterfly onto your wall.

9. Repeat Steps 2–8 with the rest of the butterflies.

Templates on page 99

BEAR BUNTING

Bring nature into your home with this beautiful Canadian-inspired bunting. To create more variation, trace the shape of the flags, then draw and cut your own design. You could develop the theme with mountains and rivers.

TOOLS

- Craft knife
- Cutting mat
- Hole or screw punch

MATERIALS

- Card, 160gsm (60lb)
- String or ribbon, maximum 3mm (⅛in) width

1. Download and print the Bear Bunting templates onto your chosen card, or use one of the other methods on pages 14–15 to transfer or trace the design.

2. Starting with the bear design, cut out all of the small grey areas within the bear that make up the fur, ear and eye.

3. Now cut out the grey areas around the bear's legs, using a ruler to cut along the straight edges.

4. Cut out the grey areas at the top of the design surrounding the trees, making sure you cut along the edges last. Carefully remove the offcuts to reveal the design.

5. Using a hole or screw punch, or your craft knife, cut out the two circles at the top of the template. Now cut along the outline to finish the flag.

6. For the tree design, cut out the smaller grey areas within the trees.

7. Then cut from the left of your template across, removing the top middle section last as this is the most fragile.

8. Cut out the two holes, then, using your craft knife and ruler, cut along the outline and remove your design.

9. Finally, repeat the template to create the desired length of bunting, and thread your chosen string or ribbon through the holes.

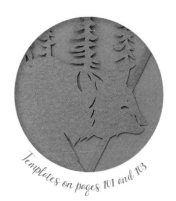

Templates on pages 101 and 103

BIRD AND FEATHER MOBILE

This eye-catching mobile will make a statement in a child's room, but would be just as stunning hung in any room in the home.

TOOLS

• Craft knife

• Cutting mat

• Hole or screw punch (optional)

MATERIALS

• Card for the birds, minimum 160gsm (60lb)

• Card for the feathers, minimum 160gsm (60lb)

• Thread or twine

• Mobile kit or branch

1. Download and print the Bird and Feather Mobile templates onto your chosen card, or use one of the other methods on pages 14–15 to transfer or trace the design.

2. Starting with the two-dimensional bird, cut out all of the small details on the wing and chest, as these are the most fragile. Then move on to the long, curved grey sections on the wing and tail of the bird. It is easiest to cut from the point on both sides of the shape and then join them up with the curve afterwards.

3. Cut out the circles, either by hand or with a hole or screw punch. Then cut around the outline of the design and remove the bird from the surrounding card.

4. Move on to the other two bird designs, using the same technique to cut out the small detail, holes and curved shapes. Using your craft knife and ruler, cut the long slit for the wings. Then cut freehand around the outline of the design.

5. To cut the wings, cut out the small pointed shapes first. Then carefully cut along the outline of the template.

6. To cut the feathers using the templates on page 109, carefully cut out the long grey line in the centre of the feather and then the small hole for the thread. Cut along the outline of the feather template.

7. Simply cut your thread to the desired length for each bird and feather, then thread through each hole and tie in place. You can then tie the elements to your mobile or branch.

Templates on pages 103 and 109

CAKE TOPPER

Add a touch of spring to your cake with these fresh-looking flower and leaf toppers. Perfect for all occasions, especially birthdays, weddings and anniversaries.

TOOLS

- Craft knife
- Cutting mat
- Bone folder
- Metal ruler
- Glue gun
- Pencil

MATERIALS

- Card for the leaf cake topper
- Card for the flowers
- Card for the leaves
- Dowel rods, 4mm (⅛in)
- Trimmed dowel rods/ flat-ended toothpicks

Templates on page 101

1. Download and print the Cake Topper templates onto your chosen card, or use one of the other methods on pages 14–15 to transfer or trace the design.

2. Cut out the large leaf design. Don't be too worried about being accurate, as all leaves are different. Now score along the centre of each leaf using a bone folder and ruler, and carefully fold the leaves slightly.

3. Cut out the flower buds. Place a small amount of glue on the back of the leaves' green spikes and glue the buds in place.

4. Measure out how high on your dowel rods you want your leaf design to be and mark it with a pencil. Place a small amount of glue on the markings you have made and roll the ends of the design around the rods to stick them in place.

5. Cut along the outlines of the flowers for the smaller cake toppers and score down the centre of the petals using your bone folder and ruler. Gently fold the petals to give a realistic look.

6. Cut out the yellow centres for the flowers and carefully bend the filaments upwards. Place a small amount of glue underneath and glue to the centre of your flowers.

7. Glue the base of your flowers and stick them to the top of your dowel rods or toothpicks.

8. Cut along the outlines of the leaves, then score a line down the centre of the leaves. Using a pencil, mark on the dowel rods or toothpicks where you would like to place the leaves. Finally, dab a small amount of glue on your markings and glue the leaves in place.

FEATHER PLACE NAME

Use this elegant feather place name to seat your guests on a special day. This design is relatively simple, so you can create multiples without taking up too much of your time. For an alternative use, you could glue the feather to a toothpick to make a cupcake topper.

TOOLS

• Craft knife

• Cutting mat

MATERIALS

• Card for the feather

1. Download and print the Feather Place Name template onto your chosen card, or use one of the other methods on pages 14–15 to transfer or trace the design.

2. Cut out the small grey areas within the feather design, including the long line in the centre. Place the tip of your blade on one of the points of the shape, then pull your blade in one smooth motion round to meet the next point. Repeat on the other side to complete the shape.

3. The bottom, more detailed part of the feather is the most fragile, so cut along the outline from the centre of the feather outwards, to create the curved lines and points.

4. Cut the 'V' shapes along the outline, cutting from the outline of the feather inwards, towards the points.

5. Cut along the rest of the outline in order to release the feather from the card.

6. Finally, write your guest's name on the solid part of the feather.

Template on page 109

FOX AND HARE LANTERN

Practise your cutting skills with this countryside lantern. The use of tracing paper creates a beautiful soft light, perfect for a lovely summer's evening.

TOOLS

• Craft knife
• Cutting mat
• Metal ruler
• Bone folder
• Glue gun or stick

MATERIALS

• Card for the lantern, 160gsm (60lb)
• Vellum paper/tracing paper
• Twine or ribbon
• Battery-operated faux candle

1. Download and print the Fox and Hare Lantern template twice onto your chosen card, or use one of the other methods on pages 14–15 to transfer or trace the design.

2. Start by cutting along the outside line of the lantern, then cut out the two grey rectangles to the left of the template.

3. Now, using your bone folder and ruler, score along all of the dotted lines and fold them. This is easier before you start cutting, as the piece is solid and less fragile.

4. Open up your lantern. For the hare design, cut out the smallest grey-shaded areas, such as the nose and eye. Continue cutting out the design from the top and working your way down, to avoid any catching or tearing. Use a ruler to help you cut neatly along any straight edges.

5. Move on to the fox design. Cut out the smallest grey areas, including the ear, eye, nose and tip of the tail.

6. As with the hare design, continue cutting out the grey areas from the top of the template downwards.

7. Once all of these areas have been cut, repeat Steps 1–6 on the other half of your lantern.

8. Now cut out four rectangles from your vellum or tracing paper, each measuring 6.5 x 10cm (2½ x 4in). Place small dabs of glue inside the lantern on each corner of the windows. Carefully stick your paper in place. This will be hidden when the lantern is complete.

9. Slot the tabs from one half into the holes of the other to join them.

10. Fold three of the sides to create an open square, then lift up the bottom tabs and place a small amount of glue underneath, to glue the tabs to each other.

11. Slot the remaining side tabs into the last two holes. Fold the small tabs at the top of the template and place a small amount of glue on them. Secure to the inside of the large tab.

12. Create a handle by tying your twine or ribbon to the two semi-circles on top of the lantern. To complete, place your faux candle inside.

Template on page 111

LAYERED STAG ARTWORK

This papercut may look difficult to make at first glance, but when broken down into layers, the shapes are relatively simple.

TOOLS

• Craft knife
• Cutting mat
• Spray adhesive
• Screw punch (optional)
• Ruler

MATERIALS

• Card for floral top layer
• Card for mountain layer
• Card for background
• 20 x 25.5-cm (8 x 10-in) frame

1. Download and print both layers of the Stag template onto your chosen card, or use one of the other methods on pages 14–15 to transfer or trace the design.

2. Trim your background card to the size of your frame, if necessary, and set aside.

3. Start with the mountain layer. Cut out the small grey areas on the top of the mountains, then cut out the river.

4. Now cut along the outline of the mountains. Then, using your craft knife and ruler, cut along the outlines to create the border. Lay the mountain layer face down on scrap paper, spray with adhesive and glue to the middle of your background card.

5. For the top layer, cut out all of the leaves in the trees, placing the tip of your blade on the point of the leaf and pulling towards the other point in one smooth motion. Repeat on the other side and remove the leaf.

6. Cut out the small grey areas on the bark of the tree. Then move on to the rest of the design.

7. Cut out the holes in the centre of the flowers with a screw punch, or using one of the circle-cutting techniques on pages 20–21.

8. Then cut and remove the rest of the grey sections within the template. Once you have removed them, cut along the outline, including the stag. Use your ruler and craft knife to cut along the border.

9. Lay the stag layer face down on scrap paper and spray with adhesive. Glue in place over the mountain layer and secure in your chosen frame.

Templates on pages 113 and 115

FLOWER PICTURE

The three-dimensional flowers and leaves give a lovely depth to this piece of art. You can multiply the flowers as many times as you want, or even scale them up to create beautiful 3-D flowers for your wall.

TOOLS

- Craft knife
- Cutting mat
- Metal ruler
- Bone folder
- Glue gun or stick
- Hole or screw punch (optional)

MATERIALS

- Card for each flower
- Card for the background
- Card for the leaves
- Card for the centres

Templates on pages 117 and 119

1. Download and print the Flower Picture templates onto your chosen card, or use one of the other methods on pages 14–15 to transfer or trace the design.

2. To make the daisy, start by cutting along the outlines of the three largest daisy shapes and the three smaller, more pointed shapes on page 117. Now, using your ruler and bone folder, score a line lengthways down the centre of each petal of the daisies and fold slightly to make the petals look realistic.

3. Now place a small amount of glue in the centre of the largest daisy shape and place the next biggest piece on top. Repeat this process with the next four shapes. Cut out the smaller circle and glue it to the centre of the daisy to complete it.

4. To make a slightly different version of the daisy, trace or print the three largest and more rounded daisy shapes on page 117, score along the petals and glue each piece together as in Step 3. Then cut out the larger circle and glue it into the middle. You can then go even further and use a hole or screw punch to cut smaller circles, which can then be glued to the centre circle, but this is optional.

5. For the final flower, cut along the outline of the two flower shapes on page 119 and glue the smaller piece to the larger. Now cut out the two centre pieces and glue them to the middle of the flower, largest first. You can then gently fold the petals and centre pieces upwards to make them three-dimensional.

6. Now move on to the leaves. Simply score along the dotted lines using the ruler and bone folder, then cut along the outline. Fold the leaves slightly. Make as many leaves as you like, to fill up the frame.

7. Cut your background card to fit the box frame. Decide where you would like your flowers to go and glue them in place on your background. Then, place a small amount of glue underneath the ends of the leaf stems and glue them in place, making sure the ends are covered by the flowers. Now secure in your box frame.

HUMMINGBIRD GLASS DECORATION

This beautiful bird decoration perches nicely on the rim of a wine glass. For a twist, make several of the birds and write a name on the solid parts, transforming them into unique place names for a special occasion.

TOOLS

- Craft knife
- Cutting mat

MATERIALS

- Card for the bird

1. Download and print the Hummingbird template onto your chosen card, or use one of the other methods on pages 14–15 to transfer or trace the design.

2. With your template on the cutting mat, start by cutting out the two long grey lines at the top of the wing.

3. Now cut out the curved grey lines underneath the wings. Place the tip of your blade at the top of the curve and pull down in a smooth motion to the bottom point. Repeat on the other side to complete the shape.

4. Move on to the semi-circles on the chest and wing, using the same technique as in Step 3.

5. Finally, cut around the outside line and remove the hummingbird from the surrounding card.

6. Now the bird is ready to place onto your wine glass. Depending on the thickness of your glass, you may need to trim a bit extra from the slit to fit.

Template on page 109

SUCCULENTS

These beautiful succulents can be displayed in many ways. Make multiples and place them in a terrarium, or display them in small terracotta pots for a more natural look.

TOOLS

• Craft knife

• Cutting mat

• Rounded pencil

• Glue gun

MATERIALS

• Card

• Flat-topped toothpicks or dowel rods

1. Download and print the Succulents templates onto your chosen card, or use one of the other methods on pages 14–15 to transfer or trace the design. Starting with the pointed leaf succulent, trace out all of the shapes four times onto your chosen card, so that you have a total of 16 shapes.

2. Cut out all of the shapes. Take your pencil and roll the tips of all the leaves around it to create a curve.

3. Place a small amount of glue in the middle of one of the largest pieces and stick the next largest on top. Repeat with the rest of the shapes in order of largest to smallest.

4. Place a small amount of glue on the flat end of your toothpick or dowel rod and stick it to the base of your succulent.

5. Move on to the second succulent and trace the template out twice onto your card.

6. Starting with the largest size, place the tip of your blade on one of the points towards the centre of the shape and, in one motion, cut along the straight lines towards the curve of the leaves.

7. Now cut along all of the curves until you can free the shape from the card. Set aside and repeat with the rest of the shapes.

8. Repeat Steps 3 and 4 to complete the succulent.

Templates on page 121

BEE PAPERCUT

This delicate papercut requires some patience and precision cutting, but is well worth the effort. It would make the perfect framed gift for any nature lover.

TOOLS

• Craft knife
• Cutting mat
• Hole or screw punch (optional)
• Spray adhesive (to frame flat) or double-sided sticky pads (to frame raised)

MATERIALS

• Card for the bee
• Card for the background
• Square box frame

Template on page 123

1. Download and print the Bee template onto your chosen card, or use one of the other methods on pages 14–15 to transfer or trace the design.

2. Start by cutting out the grey areas within the wings. Then move on to the grey pointed shapes that make up the fur of the bee, along with the bee's eyes.

3. Cut the border of the template, starting from the top. Cut out all of the circles first, as these are the most fragile. You can cut the circles using one of the cutting techniques on pages 20–21, or by using a hole or screw punch.

4. To cut out the middles of the more solid leaves, cut out the centre line first, then cut out the curved lines, from the tip into the centre line, to connect them.

5. Cut out all of the grey sections down the sides, and then the bottom section of the template.

6. Cut out the largest grey areas surrounding the bee in the centre, and then cut along the outline of the papercut.

7. Decide how you would like your design to be framed – either flat (see Step 8) or slightly raised from the background (see Step 9).

8. To frame your papercut flat, place the piece face down on scrap paper and spray with adhesive. Then simply stick it to your background card and secure in your frame.

9. To frame your papercut raised, simply place small pieces of double-sided sticky pads on the solid parts of the design. Flip the papercut over and stick it to your background card. This way of mounting creates beautiful shadows, giving the design a three-dimensional look. Finally, secure your papercut in the frame, and display.

TOADSTOOL GIFT TAG

These gift tags are the perfect finishing touch to any gift.

TOOLS

- Craft knife
- Cutting mat
- Hole or screw punch (optional)
- Glue stick or glue pen

MATERIALS

- Red card, for the top layer (minimum 160gsm/60lb)
- White card, for the bottom layer (minimum 160gsm/60lb)
- Brown or beige card, for the stem (minimum 160gsm/60lb)
- String, twine or thin ribbon (maximum 2.5mm/¹⁄₁₀in wide)

1. Download and print the Toadstool templates onto your chosen card, or use one of the other methods on pages 14–15 to transfer or trace the designs.

2. Cut out all of the circles within the top layer, using the circle-cutting techniques on pages 20–21, or a hole or screw punch.

3. Now cut along the outline of the toadstool, turning your paper to cut the curve. Set aside.

4. Moving on to the bottom layer (the white toadstool), cut along the outline, and set aside.

5. Cut out the stem for the toadstool. Line up the flat edge at the bottom of the top layer in the middle, making sure that the edge is overlapping by a little. Using your glue stick or pen, glue it in place.

6. Dab small amounts of glue around the circles on the top layer. Line up the final layer so that the curve at the top sits just underneath the small hole at the top of the red shape. Glue in place.

7. Thread your chosen string through the top hole and tie the tag to your gift.

Templates on page 125

76

TEMPLATES

WILDFLOWER CARD

LEAF FAVOUR BOX

PEONY FRAME

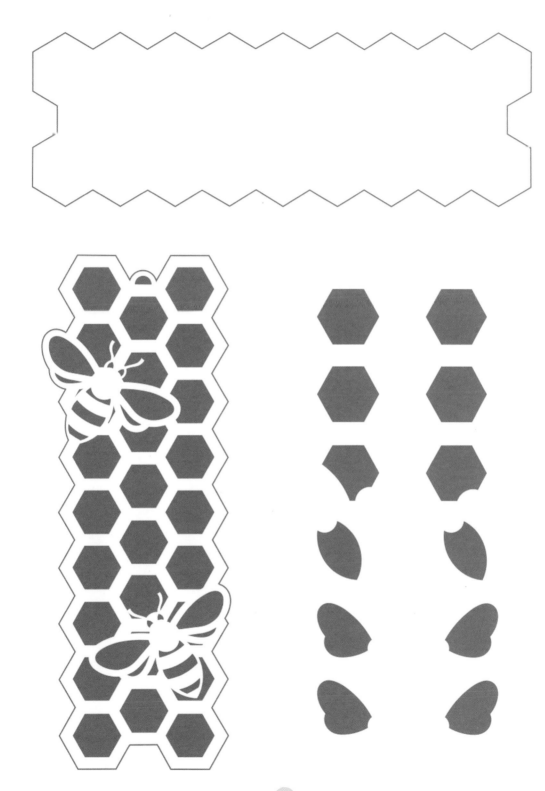

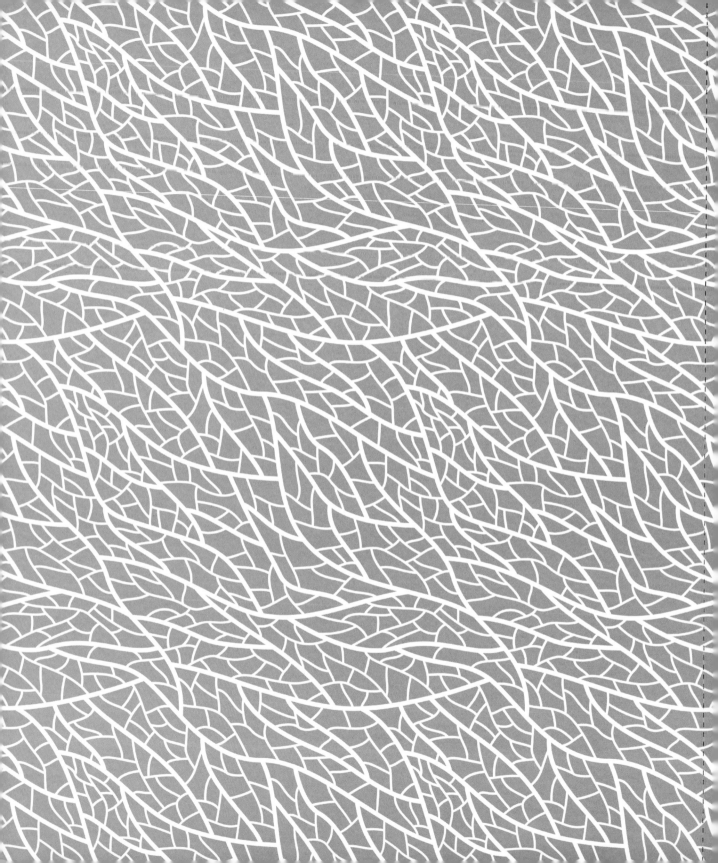

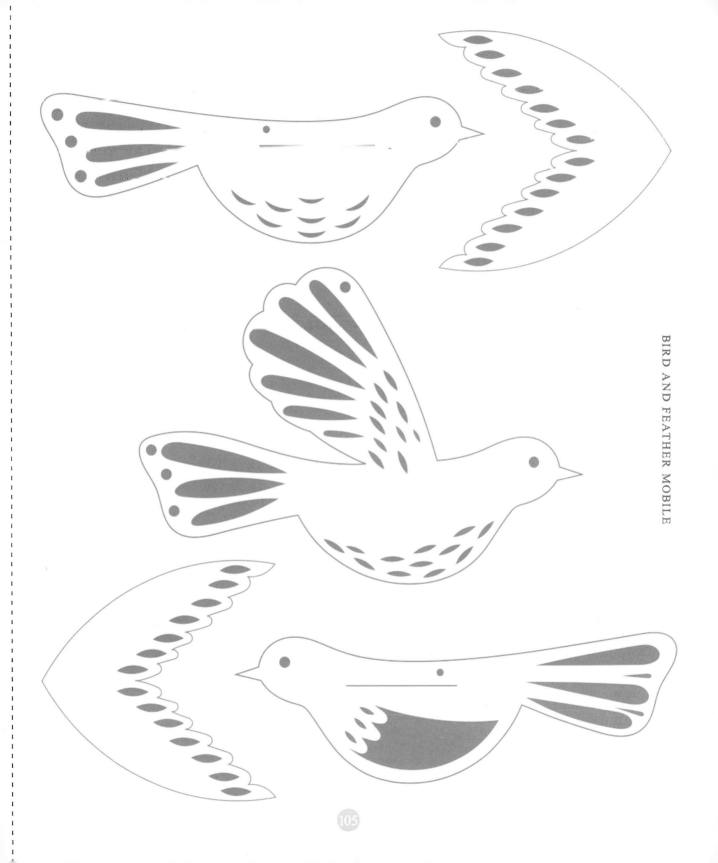

INDEX

CREDITS

I would like to thank the amazing team at Quarto Publishing for making this book possible. I never thought I would be lucky enough to have the opportunity to create my own book with my art – I am eternally grateful.

I would also love to thank my wonderful parents for always supporting me no matter what – without your help I definitely would not be where I am now. I really hope I've made you both proud! Also, to my lovely boyfriend, Tom, thank you for always being there and supporting me when I needed it most – and for that one papercut idea you've given me in over six years! Luckily for you it turned out to be my most popular. And, finally, a huge thank you to the Instagram community and to the readers of this book for your ongoing kindness.